The Doom Weaver

poems by

~~Georgia A. Popoff~~

Georgia A. Popoff

Arik
Thank you for
indulging in my vision

Georgia
9/5/08

MAIN STREET RAG PUBLISHING COMPANY
CHARLOTTE, NORTH CAROLINA

Library of Congress Control Number: 2008921250

ISBN 13: 978-1-59948-106-7

Produced in the United States of America

Main Street Rag
PO Box 690100
Charlotte, NC 28227
www.MainStreetRag.com

Acknowledgments

Grateful acknowledgement is offered from the author to the following journals for publishing earlier versions of the poems noted:

Asheville Poetry Review: "One Armed Man," "Branding," "The Doom Weaver"
Comstock Review: "Living My Dreams with Another Wife," "The Hopeful Dialect of Marriage," "Bella Luna Faccia Stellato," "On Prayer Rugs," "mango: adjective," "The Implausible Diameter of the Moon," "Heart's Desire – Cool Water"
Dharma Connection: "Worm Hole"
2001 – A Di-Verse-City Odyssey: An Austin International Poetry Festival Anthology: "Geisha"
In Praise of the Muse: Women Artists Datebook 2000: "Matrilineage"
Women Artists Datebook 2003: "Hog-Nose Adder"
Poetpourri: "Night Train"
Stone Canoe: "27 Names for Tears"
Syracuse Post-Standard: "Meteors and Delusion"
The Seasons: "Long Distance"
Worcester Review: "I Must Be Seeing Things"
X Magazine (London): "Tender Parings" (previously published online in MAP of Austin Poetry)

Web-Based On-Line Journals:

Clean Sheets: "Vengeance," "Hunger"
Poets Porch: "Animal Passion," "Tupelo Roses"

To Alexander Leon Popoff
who accompanied me
into the millennium
and taught me life…

Contents

The Geometry of Sound

Three-Faced Moon

What Remains

The Geometry of Sound

The Algebra of Poetry
The Geometry of Sound

On warm spring nights, big rigs and peepers harmonize
in the parking lot behind the Adult Ed Center, like they did
on that July evening when two teenagers crossed Euclid Avenue
lost in a loveblind poetry, the tongue's algebra.

The cosmos was settling into a simple A + B certainty.
Every house sang Houston's static love ballad.
Crackly voices seeped through the screens like incense,
and love was dense as geometry.

Physicists now proclaim that the universe
paces well beyond their expectation; one has even
substantiated God. The clouds are ripping
a ragged seam in a vast tranquil sea.

One-Armed Man

He had worked on the railroad,
his arm snatched by the larceny
of an angry train.

Fascination slowed the children
hoping to catch him at a chore
as they passed his house.

Perhaps he would be stacking
wood or mowing the grass.
That arm possessed the strength of two.

He assumed a slim angle
pushing the hand mower
across his double lot.

The neighborhood children
most liked to watch him drive.
He'd walk to the garage

short sleeve flagging
the summer breeze.
Gripping the steering wheel knob

he'd slide the car back
then glide down the black asphalt,
chrome and whitewalls gleaming.

Matrilineage
for Emma

I've never known
my great-grandmother's first name
and there's no one left
I trust enough to ask.

Her myth is a back-room whisper.
Only one picture survives.
Before my first gasp
she turned her back

on a long death
wading into snow.
Her nightgown sucked
against her ribs.
She rolled in the cold

like a cat
to encourage pneumonia,
challenging cancer
to overpower
the determined set of her jaw.

Tupelo Roses

The heat burdened bushes
in the moist Mississippi morning.
The roses in my grandmother's garden,

little slipknots and tightfisted buds,
stood up against noon.
By two they were gaping open.

The Black woman who rode the bus
south with us was quiet
and didn't object to me

using her arm as a pillow.
We took a drive past
Elvis' birthplace,

a spindly little house
on the way to the quilting factory.
My grandfather had transferred

from Manhattan to be the foreman.
His plant was on the far side of town
where faces were brown,

roads dirt-tattered,
fountains marked white and black.
The fields were shack-trimmed and full.

Fingers flurried to pick
thorny bolls while dew
still weighted the beauty

of roses in bloom, bent
backs dragging burlap tails.
My father wanted to educate me.

The adults wouldn't answer
my questions and neither did
the governor, incensed

by James Meredith's thirst to learn.
We toured factories all around Tupelo,
the last was a chicken packing plant.

At one end farmers dropped crates
of squawking birds.
Some got loose in the yard.

A tiny flame singed pin feathers off
carcasses swinging on assembly line hooks
like small pale lynchings.

We walked a steel catwalk
over a feather mountain
a bounty of white petals.

Clothes Do Not Make the Man

When the days grew butterwarm, Mother wore kid
gloves, satin soft, the pale yellow of lemon lilies.
My father's gift closed her wrists with small pearl
buttons, tear-shaped gaps displayed the silk.
Her hat brims, blatant as sun dials, cast fallen
shadows, her almond eyes forever burning.

In the basement at the foot of the stairs,
Daddy's golf shoes wait where he last left them,
like old newspapers. This season they won't be worn,
beaten rough by water hazards, sod dried in the spikes,
too many April firsts on a snowy green.

Night Train

When I was 11, Janey ushered me
to the attic and her boxy record player.
She stacked the red and black
label 45s she inherited
from her foster brothers
while our mothers drank downstairs.
She gave me James Brown
and the sanctum
I was aching for.

But she was older and the years
became territories between us.
Her roundness mimicked the ample
African woman she longed to be,
a black-fisted hair pick jabbed
in her short perm like a feather.
Janey is 45 now, her liver
lunching on itself. A train
moans through the switchyard.

Seeking the sanctuary of a bass line,
the chop of a crisp guitar,
I clean house, hop the wind
past the Bronx hospital
where Janey's last dance
is shaking the ward.
I put JB on the turntable, slide
a few steps across the living room floor,
and listen for the scream of the rails...

Miami, Florida
Atlanta, Georgia
Raleigh, North Carolina

The Reunion of False Starts

Every evening after school, after raiding
the kitchen, after sneaking young vehement sex,
after many peanut butter kisses, after nearly
getting caught a hundred times and still the risk,
long after it was time for him to be home to eat
his mother's meal, we stood wrapped on the corner
of Euclid and Fellows. Each departure, a death.

Walking backwards up the hill, flushed,
I'd watch until he turned past Sherman's store.
Which day had he stopped beyond my view
to mark our love in fresh cement?
I have searched for that tender scratch
of initials long since
suffocated by moss.

Then, last week, I saw him
and *what if* evaporated.
He had become his father; I noticed his son
strings a guitar just like he did when he
walked down Euclid Avenue singing
love songs, wires sprung from tuning
pegs with erratic, careless zeal.

The Doom Weaver

Ten Little Moons

When I was in high school
and my brother was ten,
he would hold my hand

while we watched TV.
He slid his finger over the crown
of my knuckles seeking safety

in his simple gesture.
These hands are the only parts
of me I have always loved.

Though the top skin is now less taut,
small cracks and crevices spread a web
like those on a salt flat under years of sun,

these palms are still supple.
My fingertips are ten little moons
as smooth as spoons.

I Must Be Seeing Things

Moms Mabley passed me the other day
driving a pugnosed Chevette
her face flat as the brim of her old hat

Had to be her
headed west past Blue Bros. Barber Shop
on a mission

The men in the doorway   up from their checkers
the ones sitting on the 3 green chairs
under the shade tree

missed her   though they were all
facing downtown
mouths open   talk stopped for a moment

No one else could look so much like Moms
Moving fast on Fayette   like she was late
for Ed Sullivan

Gonna miss that chance
for everybody   even me   to see her
laugh about her wrinkly husband

He was so old
he brought her back
from the dead

Living My Dreams with Another Wife

The last time we spoke
you were distracted,
late for an appointment.

You had a third child
already a toddler,
finally a daughter,
name fragrant as perfume.

25 years ago this week,
alone in a hospital
I cringed in arbitrary labor.

I was blind to what I would lose.
You compared the price tag
of freedom
to the cost of a guitar.

Now a woman near middle age,
my cumbersome body
will only bear poems.

Meteors and Delusion
for Linda and Brighton

We have shared the specter in a cow pasture
swaddled in sleeping bags like two scarabs.
With nothing but the August ocean before us, we once
watched a sluice of sparks, like catprints in snow.

This time I rose and wrapped for the cold.
I sit alone in a city and I wait for treasures.
Each phosphorous trail recalls the wide lick
of Borealis, a full moon echoing our surprise

as we melted the fall rime on the dock with our backs.
The shimmer of that green wall, the small spark of ink
guiding this poem to light, each radium soul, each loss
counted like mala beads, a November meteor mantra.
Will dawn be as haunting; will light splinter the frost?

A single yellow leaf mocks Copernicus
and falls to the ground. Several flashes
drop toward neighbors' yards. I withstand
the whistle and crunch, my mouth a crater.

Stars shatter into hot pins tattooing Orion's chest,
the count 108 like bells at New Year. I chant
to satellites, return to the house. I lock the door
on magic, shed layer after layer as I pad to find a pen.

The Implausible Diameter of the Moon

Rocks prefer to respond to gravity.
When separated from soil
it is their nature to find their way home.

I worry a pebble smooth, haunted
by a portrait on NPR years ago:
the Rwandan mother, pockets loaded

with stones to counter the ballast
of lungs, five children lashed to waist,
found bloating beneath a grieving lake.

No fish kissing sky to feed.
Their concentric screams
no longer scar the surface.

I imagine: footsteps shuffling to crib late
at night, your youngest once again teething;
the gaping crater stars cannot fill;

the eulogy for all souls bled of hope;
the mother belt I've never worn;
how satellites weep beside me.

Worm Hole

People fall in love and no one says anything about it; people burst into flame and they say, "That could never happen."

Gary Young

1.

The blue-finned Buddha is no more.
I intended to flush him but chose burial
at the last moment.
The small fighting fish, now brown,
mingles with dirt
at the foot of a young clematis.

He swims upside down in soil,
in air,
in thought.

2.

The wind sifts silt
from the white burial cloth
like powdered sugar on fried cakes
to dust those clutching the corners.

A fat pink earthworm forces to the sun.
The last trowel of dirt
is smoothed and patted ready
for the stone.

3.

This hearse
is disguised as a white Ford Escort.
Snuggled in behind the driver's seat,
five pounds of ash
in a plain brass box
wrapped in a tall kitchen trash bag.
His laugh, light as clouds,
paves the road beneath the tires.

4.

It could be a pencil box,
a place to save pennies.
It could hold bath salts
or fresh baked cookies,
chips still soft and warm.
The brass could be
pottery or wood.
The urn could be
anything.
It could have been
cheaper.

5.

Moments before the chanting
my family arrives and takes
their unfamiliar seats
in the zendo.
Hidden in a corner,
a stranger assists;
he breaks the seal with a screwdriver.
Together we pry the lid off.
There are white chips like seashells
pounded into sand
on a morning beach.

6.

The new mother, my sister,
denies we will bury
what remains of our brother.
She shares that she now feels sorry
for people who have no children.
She forgets I am empty.

7.

I pray.
Maybe I can dig
to China.

Three-Faced Moon

Hog-Nose Adder

I was born in the year of the snake.
My determined rib-cracking kick.
My ornery insistent gestation.

Deep within I carried you
captive in a fragile shell.

Had I chosen another way
we would sit together
and speak of your lunge
into the world,
your tender tear anthem.

But I was terrified of faith,
hood puffed in warning,
left eye gazing at the future,
skin like boondoggle,
fangs an omen of resolve.

I am not a woman
in my middle time
who will mourn
the final loss of breeding.

Still I rue never naming you
or answering the brittle laugh
of your rattle.

Bella Luna
Faccia Stellato

A veil whispers *cloud*,
rain little more than mist.
Mourning doves temper
dawn's brash roosters.

Sister moon, not blood
but certain twin.
Round as a wafer, her right
eye gleans knowledge.

The Tuscan sky roots
many cousins seeded
from different limbs:
surnames Nova,
Quasar, Dwarf-White.

This zenith is wild at heart.
My face reflects night peace.
Fireflies bright as planets blink
beneath my open window.

Molting Season

Unlike a snake
shedding a house
too small for its soul

I have condensed
like a black hole.
The corners of my mouth
split from cheek to ear.
This casing may crack.

The harsh sun
strips frozen rhythm
from the gourd's
robust flesh.

On Prayer Rugs

Squat at his loom, the rugmaker readies
for the incessant chant of weaving.
He adjusts the warp, fingers tightening
ordinary sisal into backbone.

He has selected wools from sheep grazed
on spring shoots, spun by virgins,
steeped in dyes drawn from beet,
onion skin, pomegranate, and blueberry.

He will blend mimosa silk into the weft,
gold and silver will exalt prayer.
He intends service, meditates
from the first sail of shuttle, left to right.

The weaver plucks and twists tufts
of color into the map of God,
the devotion of each who will sit
in supplication is set before him.

He must permit no sense
of woman praying, the curve
beneath black cotton, avoiding
her kohl-lined eyes, or flesh

untainted and soft, seated on blue
and burgundy, gold woven at his hand.
No itch should distract her delicate renewal,
no burn to grace the small of her back.

He must refuse the nectar
dream hidden in her lips
after her patchouli bath,
that tiny cask, blood warm relief.

Animal Passion

The other day
I sat across the kitchen table
from a woman whose cat rubs
against her leg after she showers.

He likes long nightgowns,
tail searching under the hem.

I confessed my male
curves around shoulders
and licks ears
the way my lover used to.

Some women choose
big dogs
to fill the hunger
their men leave,

bellies to scratch,
soft calling of names,

even the sound of *no*
a forgiveness bone.

As a Rule

I don't kill insects.
This morning I sat in the quiet sun
before the cicada had risen.
A gnat crash-landed in my cup,
drew a drop thick with cream,

a speck hoping its wings
would catch their breath.
Yesterday I saved two
bumblebees and a wasp
drowning in the kiddie pool.

The fat bumblebees
must have grown greedy with pollen,
their underbellies too delirious to fly straight.
I have no explanation for the sleek wasp
going so far off course.

One of the bees was spinning in terror.
I touched a rock to water.
He clung like algae as I placed him
in the grass and sweet clover.
This repeated until all three perched

on blades cleared of dew.
Narrow wings glistened like amber.
I will kill cockroaches.
I recognize the audacity of every person
who has hurt me as I raise my shoe.

Tender Parings

Take in hand
the finest French pocket knife,
its blade curved in a sharp grin.

Prick the skin of an August peach
near the stem but first
roll the fruit in your fingers.

Then nick it slightly, with mercy.
A tiny flap will yield
a velvet weeping heart.

Invertebrates and Retribution

A jaundiced banana slug
wends along the redwood
deck's outer crust.

          In the middle of a cornfield
          a man molded a girl's fingers
          to his pasty thickening.
          The wind turned a cold shoulder.

When threatened
the banana slug will engorge
and feign strength.

          She charted slug trails,
          dreamt of knives,
          prayed to scrub her hands
          and purge her caves with lye.

The Bearer of Grief

for Ellen

At what point
does the coconut palm
curve in sorrow,

return its arch
to the wind?
The droning sigh

of a graceful moon
accepts the impact
like a chalice.

How does the palm
anchor its path
to the sun,

its shadow on white sand
a ceiling for the spread
of blind roots?

Broad shouldered fronds
brace in reverence,
bow in pain.

Georgia A. Popoff

mango: adjective

like fruit left
on the counter too long

men embrace
a righteous grammar
covet her tenacious pit

The Fall

When I dare to be powerful – to use
my strength in the service of my vision,
then it becomes less and less important
whether I am afraid.

Audre Lorde

Eve Speaks Her Truth:

> See my sacrifice.
> Where would we all be now
>
> if I hadn't
> taken the initiative?
>
> Women bear babies in pain
> for my penance.
>
> Men ache to fill
> the darkness left behind.
>
> There was no other choice
> but to taste the future.

Adam Speaks of Apples:

> Have you ever
> noticed how much
> she smells of them,
>
> that her voice
> is as sweet as blossoms?
> My wife has my trust

and though no leaf
will hide my disgrace,
she has my love.

She shows me ways to see
in light
I was blind to before.

The Tree Speaks of Shame:

I shed paltry leaves
for my transgression,
tears falling
on dismal soil.

There is no blessing
for the instrument
of change.
No salvation.

The burden rests
in my boughs,
a dull fruit never
to meet its harvest.

Adam Speaks of Healing:

I must rise.
It is my lot
to know the power

of comfort,
to learn
compassion

and forgiveness.
To uphold the gray
god's dream.

Eve Speaks of Reflections:

His face mirrors
the scar he recognizes.

I no longer see
my image in his eyes.

I turn my head
to the burning sun.

Before First Quarter

Abstract night spreads its dark
        taut skin   the moon
        a precise scalpel   will slice
        deep into heart   leaving white blood
        splattered   stippled as stars

No place for the bold
        statement of comment   Milky Way
        No comfort   A profound incision
        rising over the hill   An errant smile
        chest laid open   before the sky blessing

Darkness will fold back   its issue
        Give new meaning   to peace
        It will be still
        just before dawn   a dog howls

Singed by Fury and the Sacred Heart

I choose joy because I am capable of it,
and there are those who are not.

Lucille Clifton

1.

The Blessed Mother was left
at my door like a discarded child.

Leaning against the cold oak
in a crinkled white bag,
her heart beacon blazed
like an angry apple.

2.

Executed with her five babies
in a rowhouse pyre,
Angel held her Baltimore corner
as long as she could.
Junkies mourned an empty minute.

3.

Some prefer to die in the dark.
Rage will sever any bond.
Incited by funereal ash
a poet cut his hair.

His locks were heavy as iron.
Stronger than Samson
he walks Brooklyn streets,
rides the subway freed of tears.

4.

The waxing moon scrapes
the bitter sky soul.
It will fatten
like a calf
inside your burning heart.

Sole Survival

Single shoes litter roads, prod concern for unshod feet.
I'm puzzled by the proliferation of such odd debris.
Confounded for years by irrational loss,
can I challenge the mystery of loafers left as waste?

I'm puzzled by the proliferation of such odd debris
just as I struggle to comprehend the nature of ice.
Can I challenge the mystery of loafers left as waste,
the premise of drumlins or the slow retreat of glaciers?

Just as I struggle to comprehend the nature of ice,
I face horror, my tragic mask of disbelief,
the premise of drumlins or the slow retreat of glaciers,
how water expanding with cold poses as bafflement.

I face horror, my tragic mask of disbelief,
turn from death to focus on a simple thought,
how water expanding with cold poses as bafflement.
There is certain diversion in confusing small details.

Turn from death to focus on a simple thought:
bloodletting is a compulsion we must reject.
There is certain diversion in small confusing details,
an escape route from our natural obsession.

Bloodletting is a compulsion we must reject.
It takes courage to turn a cheek to the side of peace,
an escape route from our natural obsession.
We are each called to accept the post of bodhisattva.

It takes courage to turn a cheek to the side of peace,
when shoes have fallen like hail and blood turned to fuel.
We are each called to accept the post of bodhisattva
at a time when hermit may seem the greater safety.

When shoes have fallen like hail and blood turned to fuel
I sift fact from fiction, seek unlikely resolve.
At a time when hermit may seem the greater safety
still I move outward, nimble, surefooted in faith.

I sift fact from fiction, seek unlikely resolve,
confounded for years by irrational loss,
still I move outward, nimble, surefooted in faith.
Single shoes litter roads, prod concern for unshod feet.

Heart's Desire –
Cool Water

I decide for the world/I decide to be born/
What will I think of this world/ What will I do
in this world/Will I be afraid of this world?

Toni Childs

1.

This is all there is to love: a wrinkle
in the fabric of water.
Lake Michigan sighs.

2.

With generous spirit, wind braids
soft smoke offerings to the elders.

3.

I threw a penny into the folds
of Bridal Veil Falls to test
the principal of falling
without fear.

4.

Benevolent as the current
of tears may seem, it is not sufficient
argument to convince me that
Ophelia accepted the perfect option.

Born Again

Every brash young poet is a martyr
conceived in the Age of Miles,
an oracle braying the news of the birth
of the cool like they knew the notes
before Miles even knew he'd blow them.

Like we never heard that shit before,
like we can't hear them sucking prana
from the lungs of saints,
their amulets and karma
tarnished by applause.

Every slick young poet bleeds
reeds instead of red,
wet with Coltrane's spit,
a moan of saxophone to measure
the weight and height of hip.

They kneel at altars
they did not dress,
impounding truth in broken
backbeats wearing their hearts
like vestments.

The Doom Weaver

The Bigamist's Wife

1.

She rises from bed center,
pads to the shower, where water
fingers the links of her back.

Nights alone she uses her left
index to lift the last drops
of gravy from her plate.

She thumbs the china lip
gingerly, a woman renewing
vows, holding her husband's hand.

2.

Does the complacent fire
eater expect to quench hunger when
he neglects embers in the stove belly?

3.

As he yanks and digs in
his heels, the good wife knows,
like the mare being gentled,
that once she stops twitching
she will bear his weight willingly.

Ballet

To dance
the snake must be clever.
To speak in tongues
she must embrace
a providence of voice
in spite of rapture.

Be a joyous snake
whose boundaries
are sterling challenges
that transcend belief.
Season earth with presence
without benefit of leg.

What Remains

The Doom Weaver

You cannot accept
the tender of my love.
Your grief waters my garden.

When sun blesses your hair
I collect strands lost to your brush,
spin gold so fine silk shivers.

Were it within my power
I would weave a shawl
on the warp of night

and protect the veiled
mirrors from the fear
in your frown.

I would bury a small box
of limitless ashes in a place
only you and I could find.

Branding

Africa was scorched into my skin at birth,
Capetown just right of my navel
then stretching melanin up my torso,
reaching the coast of Algeria
just between my tiny nipple and collar bone.

In the summer, in my sunsuit, the map I bore
darkened with middays, drew sighs from strangers.
What happened baby; were you burned?
Try to explain the continent of a birthmark at six.
My mother assured me it would fade as I got older.

My first lover was surprised to discover
the cartography of my body. We were young
and I indulged his touch and wonder, having grown
acceptance and love for the waning tone
of soft brown Saharan sand.

This mark may have more to do with where I've been
than who I am now; how I cry when the women of Mali
sing their celebration. How the timbre of drums
drives me to raise my arms in praise and pump the air.
How I want to place my feet in warm iron-red dust.

Time has passed, my lovers have changed,
the atlas is not longer my most obvious facet.
There is only the slightest shadow left, a Shroud
of Turin mist of brown that needs to feed
on summer sun to be certain.

I thought once about a tattoo, a small angel
on the inside of my right foot, just above
my ankle bone. I decided against the price
and arbitrary permanence.
It might have silenced the drums.

Nomads Prefer Finger Food

...Friday night at a small gallery...nouveau punks and the tragically hip. A tall emaciated bleached blonde leaned against the wall; her only comment a shock of chopped-off hair. She pouted and fingered her dog collar, staring past the other pasty faces, ignoring muffled voices, sunk into the wall like a painting. Our tribe bruised the hot air. We invaded in packs. We commanded the other clans, blinking like cats in their streetlight haloes. My hands became the topic of conversation. Two men compared notes, outlined my palms, tried to read my life. We were suddenly attached; they simultaneously took my fingers into their mouths. They sucked. They both laughed, and I let them. We cast our eyes around the room and laughed again...

The Doom Weaver

Geisha

I hold the secrets of the teahouse,
the bow of my mouth pursed,

my education initiated
before I painted my upper lip red.

I am well trained in silence.
There is art in hidden truths.

It is my station to practice poetry
and grace ceremony with purpose,

my days spent whisking tea,
preparing to anticipate your need,

suspended in a death juice.
I sleep alone inside a porcelain cup.

The Poet Dreams in Tankas

6 AM, alert
again, still no dawn. Hungry
for you, my thighs flank
a pillow. My eyes prospect
the bedroom's darkest corners.

Sleeping on your side,
the rift between your shoulder
blades the perfect place
to perch my cheek. My first two
fingers straddle your nipple.

No reason to ache
like this, yet my tongue is parched
and restless. Will salt
and ginger blend, season the
bland plague of this appetite?

Once I am, at last,
gifted with the sight and touch
of you, I will take
your right index finger deep
into my mouth, hold it tight.

The Hopeful Dialect of Marriage

I dream of Florence, hot Sunday morning
full of language thick as apricot jam.
Layered with church bells and passion
the air slipping through hand-sewn cotton
eyelet, sun gold as a wedding ring
squeezing through the shutter slats.
My skin, the whole room, glows art.

Angels in the architecture,
fluttering along red tile rooftops,
window boxes brilliant with geraniums,
angels kissing in the corners of frescoes.
In Florence, everyone must acclimate
to living with the flicker of wings.
Some dreams I've yet to sleep

my way into: an intimation of husband,
small secrets the hairs on our thighs
might whisper to each other
beneath the cool kiss of sheets
as we drift into single syllable starlight.
Basil from the garden riding a wisp
of moon glazed with the glow of Firenze.

The Mysteries Between Us

Lips that bear no synonym
or simple fact form small bergs,
a frozen renewal that melts in red rills.

Language is intuition, a glacier
before a river, the kiss of ghost speech,
wood amended to prophecy.

This near speaking, spite, scrapes
our tundra until nothing
is left but the ice.

We abandon our history,
our round vowels,
the trill of consonant,

glottal touches of understanding
that need no deeper definition
than rhythm.

Two flames consume our oak
and mahogany idiom.
Words coffin our anger.

Blind Submission

A former lover
whispered *touch.*

Spat control
as sacrament.

Bound her
hand and foot.

Satin
wrapped twice.

Loosely blocked
her eyes

with silk
and shocked

with slow
tongue lashings.

Released her bonds
to harvest freedom.

She has hit
two men.

He was the first.

Vengeance

The habanero sauce bottle, pepper grinder,
both phones, your pillow, our sheets, stained

not with the opium of you
but the bitter splint and crash.

I light thick sticks of Nag Champa.
My glasses still bear you on their rims.

The cats haven't licked
themselves clean yet.

I'll buy a small bottle of Japanese musk,
wear it daily, drop tears in my bath.

I'd rather own your scent
than live its haunting.

Though you are pressed throughout
my day, my pubic hair

is purged, my labia rubbed raw.
This may bring freedom

or forgiveness, one place
no longer enslaved.

Wanton Witchcraft

She practices naughty magic.
She may inflict orgasm
on a target
time zones away
then delight in his confusion.

She dreams of newts,
points an accusing finger
to wake the dawn,
discovers her lawn
livid with amphibians.

All Blues and So Forth

to Miles and Roger

I ride these notes   sometimes
     like a horse loose in sun
A   train   moving   slowly
     out of the station
     of my truth   I ride
     to escape

Brushes on snare   stick on highhat
     tapping my heart   like the click
of the grooves in highway cement
     65 miles away from me
     any given hour   my tires
         nearly bald from the running

I've flown these notes before
     but never the liberties
     they are today   I can release
        it all   homing pigeons
     that travel a thousand miles
     dotting the air   carrying
     messages   wound in tiny vials
strapped to their legs   my myths
     my lies   I send them skyward

Aviary

On the dance floor at a party, words
press through the beat to me:
You must have been taught to dance
by a Black man.

I've always danced this way.
I ponied in white go-gos at 11,
eyes closed,
constructing my cage.

Leather casual, smooth as a crow in flight,
a tall, dark-skinned man, parts the crowd
at the front of the club, gliding through
with the stealth of a raptor.

He admires the way I dance.
I like his fade, a flying V etched in blond
from the sharp line just above his temples
pointing down the back of his collar.

I rest my hand on his like a wren.
His fingers feather my skin.
Mine is a coy smile.
His reflects subtle conquest.

It is for these men I dance: the assured.
They expect notice, stand tall.
They eye the bars, admire
the exotic plumage of birds.

Dawn Cracks the Lid

Lone women shop late at night,
shirk ex-lovers,
check out in the candy aisles.

The grocery store is a desolate treachery.
The single act of selecting a basket
blares *I only cook for guests.*

Men are so adorned now; gold loops their ears,
lassoes their necks. Pants tight, they preen well,
shaking hands, cigars too big for their mouths.

Some men will comment
You know, we're good together
noticing agreement on an appetizer.

Some men wait until after they come
to speak of wives at home keeping
the books and training the dogs.

One Black Sufi dodges bullets in the Bronx.
He calls every nine months, late at night,
to profess his guardianship.

Each dawn is a Pandora's Box. Single place settings
in the dish water, a nagging sun, an unmade bed.
Coffee for one.

What Remains

Bedpan relieved
of blood holdings.

Baby folded
into paper crypt.

Nurse snaps the lid
on the contents.

Cardboard white
as an ice cream carton.

Big enough to live.
One simple statement.

In three days
engorged breasts.

Sacred Souvenirs

Pilgrims tack faith on their holy relics.
St. Catherine's fingers are ensconced in Siena;
her head fills a lighted vault in the wall,
stolen from Rome, returned to her rightful berth.
In Avila, Teresa's bones are venerated.

Still soft and warm as your infant hands,
palm to palm, I kissed you
finger by finger like rosary beads.
I wanted to lop one off, keep it in my pocket
for when I grow weak, like a rabbit's foot.

Now you linger among the desperate roses
comatose in their beds,
rescued from the drugstore dumpster;
like you, deliberating choices.
I could not save your blood in a bottle

so I write in red ink to keep you close.
Each nib stroke a breath, each word
resounds your pounding heart,
a tiny tympani beats a relentless
thunder on the roof.

Hunger

Speak to me of poetry
the way words tattoo
a blue love in summer swelter
Lavish roses
        the bold spike
        of gladiola

Before there is intimacy
        imbedded
        in your metaphor

Before you write me blue
        with ink
pressed from berries
        big as buttons

Leave a haiku
        in such small space
        as navel

Spread sonnets
        on each thigh
before your lips
are typewriter keys
kissing poems onto me
        onion skin soft
or your fingers
search the Braille
        of my toes

Milk words from the breast
of your dearest muse
       and then

Bathe me in their power
until my lips turn blue
       from wanting

Thunder Child

These are the times I feel like a witch.
Mommy taught me to respect storms; once
she outlined the details of surviving a tornado.

The boarder downstairs is confounded when I ask
to crack the window. There is no time for physics lessons.
I see the green sky and the leaves turning their backs.

The wind has stalled and circled back
three times in a half hour.
My body divines a twister is closing in.

I'm compelled to stand on the roof – it is my legacy.
Nana would rinse my tender scalp with water from the rain
barrel; my hair has been baby soft ever since.

When I drive at night, streetlights go out.
They just blink off as my car approaches.
I have grown used to it.

Then they started turning on again.
Of course there are skeptics
but I've had a witness. I terrified him.

Long Distance

To resist calling

> I hone the row of knives
> neglected in the wood block,
> the small Sabatier
> I use to core fresh cherries.

To walk away from the phone

> I water the basil a half hour
> before I cut the stems
>   with a sharp knife.
> They stand at attention
>   before they bleed,
> then I hang the bundle
> by their ankles
>   to dry.

So I won't offer another foolish plea

> I cook myself
> pasta and pudgy tomatoes,
>   flat palms of basil,
> garlic minced with vehemence.

To escape waiting for the ring

> I slip between cool sheets
> and sleep uneasily,
> dream of chopping vegetables
> for a wedding feast.

My hand on the phone

> I eat a single slice of crow
> white and bitter as a radish.

Yasoda Takes a Bite of the Infinite

I am the basis of flavor in everything. I am all
opulence. I am in the planets…I am the pure
fragrance of the earth and I am the light in all
fire. I am the life span, I am the strength. I am
the cause of everything.

Lord Krishna, the Bhagavad Gita

Krishna chews with his mouth open.
In the cavern behind my son's lips
I glimpse the universe.

No purpose other than now,
little desire for direction,
I am suddenly boundless as galaxies.

The taste of knowledge doomed Eve.
Curry stars careen and sluice
in the mouth of God.

Were moksha mine I would see
my soul housed deep in the limits
of this peckish body.

My life is meant for simple ways,
the seasons of terror.
I have no business sampling such fire.

Weights Never Carried

The precise moment loving you becomes a casket.

The satin strapped ankle and clunky toe of ballet.

The hand's carbon cargo prior to vows.

Oroboros' golden strangle on left ring finger.

A husband's New Year's Eve kiss.

The shortened breath and bladder press of fetus.

A persistent pucker on milk-fed breasts.

The tingle of phantom limb, excepting one radius

abruptly split in two by rude encounter with ice.

Trigger's enraged pulse erasing all reason.

Shovels full of topsoil to carve a roadside grave.

The first step into suicide's frontier.

A day laden with too few words.

Persecution's necktie.

My lifeless child's floppy head.

Escape from recalling the strain lifting a small rack

of bones from wheelchair to bed.

The furrow a coffin digs into shoulder.

A locust cloud's voracious appetite.

Silence so pervasive the world is rendered deaf.

With Gratitude

Many have contributed to the evolution of these poems. In particular, I would like to thank the five trusted editors whose input forced me to ask the difficult questions and achieve the deeper truth. Heather Long and Cheryl Latif guided the earliest stages of the manuscript with strength and vision. Marj Hahn also posed challenges that pushed the work into greater form. To hone it to a keen edge, I relied upon the skills and vision of Quraysh Ali Lansana and Keith Flynn, who offered much sweat equity and critical thought to the development and completion of this project as they pushed me to strive for deeper craft. Thank you all dearly.

Cathy Gibbons has added her talent to this book with her vision for the front cover. I am honored. Stephen Wright has captured my essence in a photo and I am pleased. Thanks also to M. Scott Douglass for providing this collection a home.

I also express gratitude to the members of many workshops who first responded to the poems; the journals that have chosen my words for their pages; to Phil Alexander, Chris Beck, Dale Davis, Vita DeMarchi, Betsy DuBois, Peggy Flanders, Eve Forti, Peter Goetz, Brian Goldblatt, Ryfkah Horowitz, Stazja McFadyen, Ellen McNeal, Phil Memmer, Shari Mirman, Dawn Penniman, Phil Platcow, Michael Sickler, Harvey Stein, Sue Stonecash, and Cheryl Wilkins-Mitchell for support, insight, and strength in my attaining the goal. I appreciate Ellen Bass, Quraysh Ali Lansana, and Charles Martin for their long look and comments. Lastly, thanks to John Phillips because I owe him one.

About the Author

As a teaching artist, Georgia Popoff has presented workshops at poetry festivals, in schools, after-school programs, adult education centers, community centers, women's shelters, day camps, juvenile detention facilities, museums, and teachers' in-services. Georgia has been a coach for the NAACP ACT-SO program for African American teens since 1994. In 2001, she facilitated a week-long workshop for poets in Tuscany. Georgia is also as a member of the teaching staff for the Downtown Writer's Center, the Syracuse chapter of the YMCA Writers Voice program, and for 2 years was director of a summer expressive arts program that she designed for the YMCA Camp Iroquois day camp serving nearly 1,200 children annually. Within the teaching artists' community, Georgia is a board member of the Association of Teaching Artists (www.teachingartists.com) and is Central New York Program Director for Partners for Arts Education (www.arts4ed.org), an agency providing funding and support for teaching artists, schools, teachers, and cultural organizations. Since 2006, Georgia has been the Writer in Residence for the Middletown, NY Enlarged Central School District. Georgia is a senior editor for *The Comstock Review* (www.comstockreview.org) and was poetry editor for *Central New York Environment* for 5 years. She competed in the 1994 and 1995 National Poetry Slams; poems have appeared in numerous journals, including *Asheville Poetry Review, Dharma Connection, Light of Consciousness, Midwest Poetry Review, Poetpourri, Red Brick Review, Salt Hill Journal, Worcester Review,* as well as the anthologies *The Waist is a Terrible Thing to Mind: A Wake Up Call* (Breakthrough Press, 2000); *Poetry Slam: The Competitive Art of Performance*

Poetry (Manic D Press, 2000); *2001 Di-Verse-City: Poets of the Austin International Poetry Festival;* and the Syracuse Cultural Workers' nationally noted *Women Artists Datebook* in 1998, 2000, and 2003. Her first collection of poetry, *Coaxing Nectar from Longing,* was published by Hale Mary Press in 1997 and she has been included in the Pudding House Publications' *Gold: The Greatest Hits* chapbook series (www.puddinghouse. com). Web-based publications include *poets4peace, MAP of Austin Poetry, The Poet's Porch, The Writers' Hood,* as well as moderating an ongoing on-line poetry workshop with participants from the U.S., Canada, the U.K., and Australia.